THE CANADIAN LIMERICK BOOK

But before, gentle reader, you look,
   Be advised in advance
   Of our lecherous stance
And the four-letter licence we took.

HUGH OLIVER and KEITH MACMILLAN

General Publishing Company Limited
Don Mills, Ontario

THE CANADIAN LIMERICK BOOK

Hugh Oliver
Keith MacMillan

Illustrations by Roy Condy

First published 1975 by General Publishing Company Limited

Acknowledgements:
Lots of Limericks, copyright © 1961 by Louis Untermeyer.
Reprinted by permission of Doubleday & Company, Inc.

The Lure of the Limerick by William S. Baring-Gould.
Copyright © 1967 by William S. Baring-Gould. Used by permission
of Clarkson N. Potter, Inc.

The Limerick, by G. Legman, Bell Publishing Company, © 1969.
By permission of David E. Seham Associates, Inc.

Design: Brant Cowie/Artplus
Illustrations: Roy Condy

ISBN 0-7736-1018-9
Printed and bound in Canada by
T.H. Best Printing Company Limited, Don Mills, Ontario

Introduction: Part One

In General ...   The cult of the limerick dates back at least a hundred years. During that time, the limerick's popularity has waxed and waned, but today it seems to be flourishing as heartily as ever. Its appeal extends from the most sophisticated intellectual to the coarsest backwoodsman, though it is generally enjoyed more by men than by women. And its relatively simple and well-defined structure encourages its creation by people who would otherwise not attempt to set down a line of verse; one does not have to be a poet to write good limericks, although many well-known poets have written them.

In essence, the limerick is a five-line verse with a strict metrical and rhyming form. The content is that of a story reduced to skeleton proportions. As a general rule (to which there are many exceptions), the first two lines set the scene — they introduce a character and say something about him.

There was a young man of Eau Claire
Enjoying his girl on the stair;

The next two lines are concerned with action—they describe what the character does or is done to him.

> *On the forty-fourth stroke,*
> *The banister broke*

The concluding line describes the consequences of the action.

> *And he finished her off in midair.*

Some limericks rely for their humour on situation, some on word play; the best generally combine the two. It is a well-known fact that the majority of the better limericks are lewd — or "unlaundered", to use the limerist's jargon. The following limerick by an anonymous author portrays this very neatly:

> *The limerick packs laughs anatomical*
> *Into space that is quite economical.*
> > *But the good ones I've seen*
> > *So seldom are clean*
> *And the clean ones so seldom are comical.*

As to one of the reasons why this should be, I should like to venture an opinion. In his penetrating analysis of humour, Henri Bergson (in his book *Le Rire*) defines a situation as comic when the person in the situation behaves inflexibly or resembles a machine. And in the limerick, where there is no opportunity in the five brief lines for any subtle character build-up, it is on the inflexible and machine-like attributes of the subject that the limerist must usually concentrate. In this context, the most obvious mechanical attribute of the human is his body and the most obvious mechanical attribute of his body in action is sex — plus, if you will, eating and elimination. Consequently, most of the better limericks are unlaundered limericks and, until a few years ago, relied on circulation largely by word of mouth. Recently, however, with the advent of a new permissiveness, many of these have now been published, and the sale of limerick books is evidence of their widespread popularity.

Limerick scholars (and there are quite a few of them) have traced back the form to such long-ago writers as Shakespeare; but for all practical purposes, the limerick can be said to start with Edward Lear (1812-1888), English artist and nonsense writer. (*En passant*, it would be convenient if the origin of the name "limerick" could be associated with the town of Limerick in Ireland. But the argument is that it is not. Nobody really knows.)

Lear, who is often referred to as the father of the limerick, wrote over two hundred of them. They are generally characterized by a last line that is a simple variation of the first, and consequently they lack the humorous punch of more modern limericks. Only one of his limericks refers to a place name that is unambiguously Canadian, and it is not one of his best.

There was an Old Man of Quebec,
A beetle ran over his neck;
But he cried, "With a needle
I'll slay you, O beadle!"
That angry Old Man of Quebec.

Because of its ethnic mix and, in particular, because of the Indian influence, Canada is extraordinarily rich in the kinds of place names — Sault Sainte Marie, Chicoutimi, Timiskaming, etc. — that challenge the virtuosity of the limerick writer. This present book explores some of the possibilities.

In Particular . . .   This book had modest beginnings. As far as I was concerned, it started in April 1966 when, as a landed immigrant, I disembarked with my family on the dockside at Montreal. At that time, a Montreal radio station was running a limerick competition, and I was thereby impelled to write the one about the stripper on page 47. However, for some reason (absentmindedness, I think, rather than modesty) I failed to send it in.

Subsequently, over the ensuing years, I continued to write more "Canadian" limericks — it can become a habit; some would argue a contagion — until I had a collection of about sixty. It was then that I began to think in terms of a slim paperback, and with a sense more of nothing to lose than of anything to gain, I mailed them in to General Publishing.

I was duly gratified when the firm showed interest, but the proposal they came up with was a great deal more ambitious than anything of mine — namely, a collection of some three hundred limericks, with a corpus of a hundred (if you will pardon such an esoteric expression) contributed by myself, and the rest culled from . . . well, nobody was too sure.

After a somewhat feverish gestation period around Christmas, I managed to write another fifty; and let me add that the treadmill process of creating limericks can be more fruitful than one might suppose because, if one waits on inspiration, she can be slow coming — as the bishop said. . . . Meanwhile, discovering sources of other limericks was proving more difficult. Likely there were lots of them stashed away, but how to unearth them? The publishers wrote to radio stations and to magazines that had formerly run limerick competitions, and they in turn ferreted through their archives, sometimes with success, sometimes without. In particular, we should like to thank the CBC's *Royal Canadian Air Farce Show* and the former *Star Weekly*, Panorama section, who put us in touch with many of the contributors included in this book. A few were without address—where are you, J.P. Slugworthy, "of no fixed abode"? We also examined other books to find limericks with Canadian place names. But after a few months, it began to seem that our target was over-ambitious. Furthermore, I was somewhat self-conscious that whereas my own contribution contained a high proportion of unlaundered limericks, the others we had managed to find, because they had been written for broadcasting or family reading, were most of them puritanically clean: by comparison, I would come across as a dirty old man, and though I may be, I did not care to have it made so publicly obvious. What would my aunt say?

It was then that we happened on a treasury of limericks that solved both problems; for Keith MacMillan emerged with the hundred or so he had written, every one of them quite as bawdy as any of mine and displaying all the dedication and polished skills of the limerist's art. This book then is made up of his collection, mine, and those we managed to get from other sources. How Keith came to write his, I leave him to tell.

Hugh Oliver

Introduction: Part Two

On reflection I realize that my contribution to this book has been gestating since childhood. My father's talent for versification was well known to his friends and the limerick was always a favourite verse form. In our family, one was expected to versify on birthdays, weddings and other family occasions and the infectious lilt of the limerick was never for long out of the ear. Once, for example, in my teens, after a mildly disastrous chemistry experiment in the basement, I was greeted with

There was a young chemist named Keith,
Who escaped by the skin of his teeth
  From H_2SO_4
  While the family bore
The explosions going on underneath.

That indefatigable composer, the late Healey Willan, a family friend, was surely one of Canada's most gleeful collectors, and creators, of limericks, the cleverer and more sullied the better ("I say, old man, have you heard the one about . . . "); he was amused, I think, by one of mine that appeared in the Toronto Telegram (suggested and polished by Clyde Gilmour) on his 80th birthday:

There was once an old Willan named Healey
From whose pen music flowed rather freely;
> *But to friends, 'twas the terse*
> *And quite secular verse*
He composed even more freely, really.

Yes, the limerick was an integral part of my background, limericks of all persuasions, including of course the distinctly off-colour.

It was about 1967 that Edith Fowke introduced me to (a smuggled copy of) the massive and unlaundered compendium of some 1,700 limericks compiled by Gershon Legman; shortly thereafter my wife gave me a copy of another priceless collection, *The Lure of the Limerick*, and limerick rhymes and rhythms began dancing in the head again. In these collections the best ones seemed always to be on foreign names, whether in England (Chichester. . . "britches stir"; Exeter. . . "distinguishing mark of his sex at her";

Worcester. . . "sedorcester"), or Brazil (Amazon. . . "pyjamason"), even Persia (". . . it's not love, it's inertia") — anywhere else, it seemed, but Canada, except perhaps for the notable, if unexciting:

There was a young man of Quebec
Who was buried in snow to his neck.
*   When asked, "Are you frizz?"*
*   He replied, "Yes I is,*
But we don't call this cold in Quebec."

by no less than Rudyard Kipling.

Around 1967, of course, the centennial year of Canadian confederation, national chauvinism was running high. One evening, upon being challenged to write a limerick on "Chicoutimi", I was suddenly aware of the vast panorama of the Canadian place names waiting there untouched, virgin — Argentia, Port aux Basques, Antigonish, Tatamagouche, Musquodoboit, Matapedia, Shawinigan, Jonquières, Métabechouan, St. Benoit du lac, Ontario, Timiskaming, The Sault, Portage la Prairie, Saskatchewan, Wascana, Batoche,

Banff, Quesnel, Sicamous, Kootenay, Kamloops, Spuzzum, Vancouver — the list is endless, and irresistible! And so started the systematic realization of a (I hoped) unique collection of limericks stimulated by such Canadian place names. It grew, paused, grew some more, paused again, and finally, when it was nearing the target of 101, I heard through the publishers' grapevine of the similar collection Hugh Oliver had not only written but was preparing, supplemented by many others from various Canadian sources, for publication by General Publishing. *Mirabile dictu*, he was looking for yet another hundred or so — and here were mine! Never was a collaboration more natural, more inevitable and more enjoyable.

The Topsy-like growth of this book has resulted, of course, in a somewhat odd assortment — about one third Oliver, one third MacMillan and almost one third polyglot. We hope, however, that this has imparted to the whole a certain variegation — the good old Canadian "mosaic" — even though inevitably we have selected our favourites and indeed not hesitated to touch them up a bit here and there where needed. The end, after all, is not documentation but entertainment — at least for those whose tastes run to the elegantly bawdy, in true limerick tradition.

To those unfamiliar with this tradition (until very recently very difficult to find in print) we can make no apology for the prevailing raunchiness of imagery and language, since this is quite deliberate. We can and of course do regret any offence caused hereby — but we cannot apologize for it. Likewise we regret, but remain unapologetic, if this book imparts to the uninitiated the impression that we are putting down (or "sending up") the subjects of these verses, be they places, politicians, Canadian symbols or whatever. But the putdown is the very essence of the limerick form and tradition. Even so, we intend no offence to any person or place — just good, dirty fun!

During the current period of our national development, Canada and Canadians are establishing a new self-awareness and self-assertion. This modest volume in its own way is an attempt to establish *our* place of abode, Canada, in the international world of the limerick.

We hope, moreover, that it will stimulate others to do likewise. There are, for example, no limericks here on New Liskeard, Rustico, Hochelaga, Chebucto, Souris, Camrose, Fort Garry, Cayuga, Cataraqui, Campobello, Bella Coola, Asbestos, Anticosti, Lake of the Woods or (praise be) Kazabazua. Likewise the names of a few other major cities remain unviolated, too great a challenge to our feeble rhyming talents.

The challenge is there, and readers of this book, since limerick readers are usually also limerick writers, will be impelled to respond. Untouched place names and Canadian themes abound. As a glance at an atlas will show, there remain many hundreds, we know; and perhaps we'll receive, we would like to believe, maybe over a thousand or so — from which a new collection could be compiled. General Publishing will be glad to forward them to us.

Meanwhile, who can do something with:

A dirty old man of Chignecto . . .

Keith MacMillan

To my brother John
H.O.

ATLANTIC PROVINCES

A kinky old dame in St. John's
Has a thing about crustace-ons,
    Being roused by the grabs
    Of the lobsters and crabs,
As she tickles her tits with the prawns.

K.M.

To a virgin old maid of Argentia,
Said this fellow, "Can I be a frentia?"
    But she let out a yell,
    Screaming loud bloody hell
In an outburst of pre-cocks dementia.

K.M.

A Newfoundland lad from Placentia
Was in love to the point of dementia,
    But his love couldn't burgeon
    With his touch-me-not virgin
Till he screwed her by hand, in absentia.

ANON.

A fisherman, near Bonavista,
Thought he'd have an affair with his sista,
    But he turned her down cold
    When at length he was told
All the ways that his buddies had kista.

K.M.

When Cabot reached Cape Bonavista
His ship had a bit of a lista;
    But he reached for his hat
    And said "Never mind that —
Just look at that Beothuk's sista!"

Ray Goodyear, Sydney, N.S.

A young fisherman near Port aux Basques
Was too timid and bashful to asques;
    But to any young broad
    Who would fillet his cod
He would speedily rise to the tasques.

K.M.

A deflorate of old Corner Brook,
Still impaled on her gentleman's hook,
    Was impelled to remark,
    Lying there in the dark,
"It was just like it said in the book!"

K.M.

A Corner Brook citizen said,
As he looked at the clouds overhead,
    "In spite of this vapour
    We make pulp and paper
Without which this couldn't be read."

Alice M. Keys, Scarborough, Ont.

A Corner Brook man in a pub
Paid for drinks with a cod and a chub;
    But he thought it quite strange,
    When he asked for his change,
To get two pounds of smelt in a tub.

J. Bentham, Port Mellon, B.C.

A craftsman of north Newfoundland,
Upon finding his tool in demand,
    Decided to stay
    With the oldfashioned way —
And continued to make it by hand.

K.M.

Said the Newfie, undoing his coat,
"Watching TV at home gets my vote;
    Coz although it's quite nice
    When you fish through the ice,
You need such a big hole for the boat."

H.O.

There was a sweet lass of Belle Isle
Who wore a perpetual smile,
    And so did her lad,
    For it seems that they had
Special uses for cod-liver ile.

K.M.

It may have been Wayne or been Shuster,
But whichever it was it amuster
    When Shuster or Wayne
    Clambered on to a plane
And then got off at Gander and guster.

H.O.

In the fleshpots of North Labrador
Lived a fat and voluptuous whore.
    Contagiously jolly,
    They nicknamed her Olly
Because of her asking for more.

H.O.

A vigorous young Nova Scotian,
Used to plunging about on the ocean,
   By his girl was undressed
   And is now quite obsessed
With that up-and-down copular motion.

K.M.

A sculptor in far Nova Scotia
Behaved in a manner not kotia:
   When a statue of Nancy
   Excited his fancy
He used a large chisel to brotia.

H.O.

There was a young lad of Bras d'Or
Who was laid by a maid on the shore;
    It excited him blind
    When she teased his behind
While engulfing his eager before.

K.M.

A man from Cape Breton we find
Who is honoured as one of a kind,
    Since he saved on the Cape
    A young maiden from rape —
He undressed her but altered his mind.

H.O.

For a scrupulous bride of Cape Breton,
An engagement of teasin' and pettin'
    So whetted her lust
    That, when wedded, she just
Couldn't wait to begin the begettin'.

K.M.

There was a young fellow of Sydney,
Who put it in up to her kidney,
    But a jock from Quebec
    Got it up to her neck —
'Cause he sure had a dandy one, didney?

ANON.

An elder of old Halifax
Would bolster his weapon with wax
    For his wife, in the main,
    So she wouldn't complain
If he should prematurely relax.

K.M.

This guy with the girl from Dalhousie
Succeeded in making her drowsy —
    But he speedily found,
    Long before she came 'round,
That her centre of int'rest was lousy.

K.M.

There was a young woman of Chester
Who said to the man who undressed her,
    "I think you will find
    That it's better behind —
For the front is beginning to fester."

ANON.

Lay a frustrated lobster, off Chester,
With his mate, in the mood to molest her,
    Thinking, "How in the hell
    Did I get past the shell
When I *last* got the itch, and undressed her?"

K.M.

From a chef of Annapolis Royal
Comes this recipe: "Baste her in oil,
    Gently increase the heat
    Till she's tender and sweet
And then serve, *en brochette*, at the boil."

K.M.

The art-loving Bishop of Truro
Kept a nude by Renoir in his bureau;
    He explained, "It's not smut
    That engrosses me, but
Nineteenth-century chiaroscuro."

Mavor Moore, Toronto, Ont.

Said the dowager, "Fundy's the Bay,
I can revel my future away;
    For I'm longing to ride
    On the strength of the tide,
And the Fundy comes twice every day."

H.O.

A bluenose from Antigonish
Had a torrid affair with a fish;
    "I just swim in the nude
    And we couple, in lewd
Consummation, whenever we wish."

K.M.

'Twas a fellow of Tatamagouche,
Who would go, when he went, with a whouche!
    He was frequently known
    To perform all alone,
So had nowhere to squirt all the jouche.

K.M.

A philandering fellow of Pictou
Had no girl he could steadily stick to;
    None had ever enough
    Of the physical stuff
To encompass his knackers and dick too.

K.M.

Fisherfolk in the I. of P. E.
Find the sexiest things in the sea,
　　Like the softer, and moister,
　　Indigenous oyster —
Does every Malpequer agree?

K.M.

A Charlottetown matron, offended
At meeting her daughter's intended,
　　Said, "No, he won't do,
　　His nose isn't blue;
The marriage is not recommended!"

Mary Ringland, Manotick, Ont.

An impatient old man of Malpeque
Used to lay out his codpiece on spec,
    "Not to offer as bait,
    But in case I can't wait,
It's all ready and waiting on deck."

H.O.

An impotent fellow of Borden
Was accused by the lady of hoardin'
    His spermatozoa
    (Although she loved moa
The cute little things they were stored in).

K.M.

In New Brunswick, a cute little wench
Muttered, "Let us be glad for the French!
    For none of them doubt
    What the ball game's about,
While the English just sleep on the bench."

H.O.

An affectionate girl of Acadia,
To her fella said, "What can I sadia?
    That casual lay
    Was simply my way
Of a pleasant hello and good dadia."

K.M.

There was once an excessively peur
Mad'moiselle from the Bay of Chaleur
    Who had never been won,
    Till some guy turned her on
And she's now just a lecherous wheur.

K.M.

At this inn on the Miramichi
One can have any service for free —
    Table d'hote, a la carte,
    Fluffy dumplings, or tart —
If one has the appropriate key.

K.M.

A lady from Passamaquoddy
Possessed a magnificent body,
    And her face was not bad,
    Yet she'd never been had
For her odour was markedly coddy.

ANON.

A young lady of Passamaquoddy
Was addicted to hot whiskey toddy,
    Which rendered her prone;
    So she came to be known
As the earthy, but heavenly, body.

K.M.

A Mountie of old Musquodoboit
Had a pecker so long, girls would mob it,
    But the locker-room boys
    Would unsettle his poise
With their constant "long arm of the law" bit.

K.M.

If in Moncton they ask you to dine
And you're down there at fiddlehead time,
    Be ready to yearn
    To munch on some fern
Or else be prepared to decline!

T. Green, Toronto, Ont.

A lush out of Moncton called Bill
Made moonshine on Magnetic Hill.
   It "attracted" the Mounties
   From over three counties;
They just would not stand for a still.

Gordon McCully, Moncton, N.B.

A New Brunswicker, down in Saint John,
Was caressed by his girl on the lohn,
   And with consummate skill
   She engulfed him until,
With a giggle and gasp, he had gohn.

K.M.

Said a priest to a tart in Bay Shore,
"Our deportment I roundly deplore —
   'Tis original sin."
   Said the tart with a grin,
"But I've done it quite often before."

H.O.

A Fredericton frigate bird bet
A Prince Rupert pigeon he'd get
   Cross country, both ways,
   In less than six days —
Then flew it Air Canada jet.

Jim Yeates, Toronto, Ont.

QUEBEC

A grotesquely endowed Québecois
Set up house, with a squaw, dans les bois,
    For in "combat de fuc"
    He had found that her "truc"
Was a match for his "je ne sais quoi".

K.M.

An Olympian lass of Gaspé
Was acknowledged a sumptuous lé,
    And with never a fee;
    "Be divested," said she,
"Of my amateur status—no wé!"

K.M.

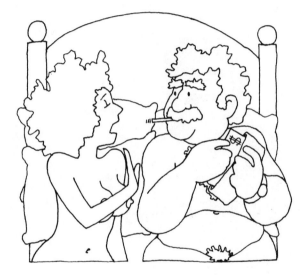

A Paul Bunyan from wild Matapedia
Shoots it into his girl, like a metia;
    "I'm just making the most,"
    He will blatantly boast,
"Of my principal salient featia!"

K.M.

An uncouth, lusty youth in Sept Isles,
I admit, is a bit of a hisles.
    He assesses a prude
    By her mood in the nude,
And a bitch by the pitch of her squisles.

K.M.

36

A musical man of La Tuque,
As he wrote his ninth Prelude and Fuque,
    Was constrained to observe,
    As he steadied his nerve,
"If I do this again I will puque!"
K.M.

While hunting for ducks in the Saguenay
An Englishman suffered sheer aguenay,
    Sitting out on a lake
    Making sounds like a drake
But in French too anguissant to baguenay.
H.O.

At ten forty-three in Arvida
The fast-working lecher first spida.
    Then at ten forty-four
    He'd his hand at the door
And at ten forty-five was insida.

H.O.

There was an old whore of Arvida
Whose pelvis grew wida and wida.
    One day, full of gin,
    Her old boyfriend fell in
And was drowned in the chasm insida.

K. M.

Said a scientist based at Shipshaw,
As he fondled the boobs of a whaw,
    "Just the press of my hand
    Seems to make you expand,
Thereby contravening Boyle's law."

H.O.

Said a ripe demi-vierge of Chicoutimi,
To her shy, loving lad, "It's all noutimi."
    But after eight starts
    At conjunction of parts
She complained, "You're just not gettin' throutimi!"

K.M.

Said an aberrant wife from Chicoutimi,
"I know what I wish men would do to me.
    But unless they can melt
    This damn chastity belt
I'm afraid that they might not get through to me."

H.O.

A nun from the town of Shawinigan
Felt an urgent compulsion to sinigan;
    So she asked the devout,
    "Will you kindly pull out
And then straightaway slip it back inigan."

H.O.

An exhausted young bride of Shawinigan
Was so pooped she just couldn't beginigan,
 Yet couldn't restrain
 Her insatiable swain
Who continued out-in-out-and-inigan.

K.M.

There's an odd sort of broad in Jonquières
Who preferred it with *everything* bare,
 And even professed it
 Was better, divested
Of *all* her superfluous hair.

K.M.

Said a father, from near Métabechouan,
To his son, "I just wanted to let you on
 To a secret, you slug —
 You are now on the rug
That your mother and I did beget you on."

K.M.

Said a virgin who lived in St. Yves,
"Pray, good sir, ere my membrane you cleave
 With your life-giving sword,
 Let me first thank the Lord
For what I'm about to receive."

H.O.

A voluptuous maid of St. Jacques
Was betopped with a generous stacques;
  And her front clearly meant
  That she sportingly spent
A good part of her life on her bacques.

H.O.

Voir le jeune matelot de Québec,
With a dong that hung down to the deck;
  So to keep it from harm,
  And to keep himself warm,
He just wound it around at the neck.

K.M.

A psychologist near Trois Pistoles,
When he studied the feminine role,
From statistics and charts,
Clearly proved that the parts
Added up to much less than the hole.

H.O.

In Quebec, that impregnable fort,
There was wild merrymaking and sport;
Cried Montcalm in alarm,
"Mes amis, vite aux armes!
There's a terrible Wolfe à la porte!"

Sylvia Mead, Victoria, B.C.

All honour and glory accrues
To the regiment of the Vingt-Deux.
  Said a girl with delight,
  "I don't know about fight
But the whole twenty-two of 'em screws."

H.O.

A mistress of chess from Quebec
Wore a blunderbuss slung at her neck.
  When a man for a caper
  Attempted to rape her,
She blew off his head and said "check!"

H.O.

Years ago it was often necessity
For political gain in Quebessity
    To grease every hand
    With a couple of grand
And other such forms of duplessity.

H.O.

A housewife from near Trois Rivières
Won awards for her buns at the fair;
    Though not for their size
    Did she garner the prize —
But their place in her sweet dairy air!

J.P. Slugworthy

A perverted young girl of Three Rivers
Gives her sisters a case of the shivers;
    Sexy spasms has she,
    Rubbing up to a tree,
And again when extracting the slivers.

K.M.

The seamen who sail the St. Lawrence
View the river in utter abhawrence,
    Coz it isn't too nice
    To be battered by ice
Or to drown in the vicious cross-cawrence.

H.O.

In the turbulent turgid St. Lawrence
Fell a luscious young damsel named Florence,
    Where the poor famished fish
    Made this beautiful dish
An object of utter abhorrence.

ANON.

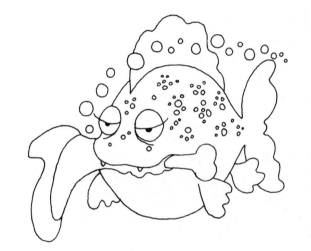

I recall a young man of Sorel
Who could cause his saliva to gel;
    And whenever he came
    He could do just the same
With his seminal fluid as well.

K.M.

One musical chap of Champlain
Painted keys on his lovely Hélène.
    Improvising in C,
    When he fingers low G
She da capo's, again and again!

K.M.

A fragile young maid from Brome Lake
Was obsessed by the fear she might break,
    But succumbed in the end
    To the plea of a friend
That "I promise to mend what I make."

H.O.

'Twas a monk of St. Benoit du lac
Whose libido was 'way out of whack.
    Once, molesting a nun,
    He had scarcely begun
When he found he'd forgotten the knack.

K.M.

This weirdo outside Montreal
Had to pee in a pot in the hall.
    As he stood there, said he,
    "I've a problem, you see,
With this huge unpre-emptible ball!"

K.M.

Deux amants sat in old Outremont
In a charming, intime restaurant.
    Said she, panting, "J'ai faim,
    Donne-moi coq-au-vin,"
So he did! N'est-ce pas que c'est bon?

K.M.

A stripper in Old Montreal
Allowed her last fig leaf to fall.
    Said the maître de strip
    "You must tighten your grip
Parce qu'il n'est pas permis montrer all."

H.O.

A whore on St. Catherine Street
Her client rebuked in some heat:
  "Kindly pay what it's for,"
  She said to him, "or
Round my bush you may no longer beat."

H.O.

You'd be wise not to look with disdain
Through the windows of Château Champlain.
  Though they offer, 'tis true,
  A half-circular view,
Better half of a glass than no *pain*.

H.O.

A naive student nurse of McGill
Made excessive demands on the Pill
    When six interns she'd bed
    Every night, 'cause they said
It was part of the hospital drill.

K.M.

Then a middleaged man of McGill,
Much afraid he was over the hill,
    Came once more with his hand
    And some extract of gland
Plus a strenuous effort of will.

K.M.

Jean Drapeau, though a dreamer perchance,
Can envisage his city's advance
    Till it spreads all the way
    Up to far Hudson Bay
And the Metro's connected to France.

H.O.

When questioned concerning her view,
A tourist replied that she knew
    The meaning quite well
    Of the letters FL
And would relish a stab at the Q.

H.O.

An old spinster outside Saint Jérôme
Had a shameful affair with a gnome,
    Who was so oddly hung
    That she hid him among
All the junk in the cellar at home.

K.M.

To ski down the snowy Laurentians
Went a girl with the best of intentions;
    But her skiing instructor
    Downed ski poles and fuctor
And other things nobody mentions.

H.O.

Un jeune homme de Ste-Anne-de-Bellevue
Demandait à les filles, "Screwez vous?"
    Il sourit, quand les belles
    (Ou même n'importe quelles!)
Répondaient, en effet, "Oui, we do!"
K.M.

A maiden called Anne that I knew
Was distressingly wedged up the flue,
    Where she died out of shame
    Canonized by the name
Of the lovely Ste. Anne de Bellevue.
H.O.

There was a young maid from Lachine
To whom sex in a car was obscene.
    But I ought to explain
    That she liked it by train
And was screwed on the seven fifteen.

H.O.

There was a young girl of Lachine
Whose response was excessively mean.
    Though she was, they all said,
    Rather stingy in bed,
She at least was dependably clean.

K.M.

Said the Sieur de la Salle, "Let us pray
That we make it to China today.
    It's a good sign we've been
    Several leagues past Lachine
And have met not one maudit Anglais!"

F.P. Hughes, Hawkesbury, Ont.

A slothful young fellow from Hull,
When life seemed excessively dull,
    Once tried thinkful wishin'
    With slow manumission —
But dropped off to sleep in a lull.

K.M.

ONTARIO

An eccentric young man of Ontaria,
Once announced to his genital varia,
   "I have knitted this red
   Woolly snood for your head,
With a pocket for each of the paria."

K.M.

To play was a young lady's dream
With the Ottawa Rough Rider team —
   Inside guard or full back,
   On defence or attack,
In an orgy of mud and whipped cream.

H.O.

An unfortunate marksman from Ottawa
Had his masculine trophies all shottawa;
    And the girl he adored
    Very quickly grew bored
And although he pursued her she gottawa.

H.O.

Said a forward young patient from Madoc
To her G.P. "You've got quite a wadoc;
    And if able you are
    Then I might go so far
As to sadoc you madoc me ladoc."

H.O.

Said a nun from the town Gananoque,
"All the clergy I hold in obloque;
    For a priest made a pass
    At me during mass
And a bishop once tried to unfroque me."

H.O.

An inmate of Kingston's old pen
For freedom developed a yen;
    He got over the wall
    With no trouble at all,
By sheer levitation and Zen.

R.S., Sudbury, Ont.

A deer hunter near Napanee
Went around camouflaged as a tree,
    When a squirrel with guts,
    Having chewed off his nuts,
Stored 'em deep up his posteritee.

H.O.

A generous lass of Port Hope,
Disliking both liquor and dope,
    To make the thing easy
    (And slightly more teasey)
Would line the whole passage with soap.

K.M.

There was once an old lady of Bewdley,
Who would *never* do anything crudely!
    But her fantasy life
    Was especially rife
With machismos who screwed her quite lewdly.

K.M.

A young hippie from Oshawa, Ont.,
When arrested for filling the font,
    To the magistrate said,
    "The old values are dead!
We are free now to pee where we want!"

K.M.

A preposterous fellow of Whitby
Had no clue as to what could the clit be,
    But imagined he thought
    That he *sort* of knew what
Could that thing at the tip of the tit be.

K.M.

There's an unbroken babe in Toronto,
Exceedingly hard to get onto,
    But once you are there
    And have parted the hair,
You can revel as much as you wanto.

ANON.

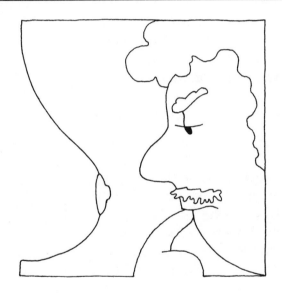

As Toronto's incredible spire
Stands up to the clouds and much higher,
    The men feel dejection
    Before this erection
While women go wild with desire.

H.O.

A delicate schoolboy on Yonge
To a bodyrub parlour was brung,
    Where a topless Malay
    So massaged him away
That she left him with only his. . . well, I think
    it was his tongue. *H.O.*

One virginal lass from Toronna,
Invited to sex, said "Dowanna;"
    Said her suitor, "O bully!"
    He understood fully
The value she placed on heronna.

James Gayfer, Dartmouth, N.S.

A young lassie from Bathurst and Queen
On the use of the Pill was quite green;
    "It protects me, they say,
    Every time that I lay —
But it keeps dropping out, in between!"

K.N

The Argonauts' priest was heard say
To the big Double Blue — "Let us pray
    That disease and fatigue
    Strike the rest of the league
And we may win the Grey Cup some day."

H.O.

Said the Archer with due modesty,
"If Toronto you're coming to see,
    And you have time to spare,
    Take a stroll through the square —
Watch the people watch people watch me."

Alan M. McLachlin, Waterloo, Ont.

Said a fanciful frump from Toranda
"There's a foible I've kinda got fonda —
    When I hear a new name
    Of a guy or a dame,
I pernounce it the way that I wanda."

J.P. Slugworthy

One sweet damsel of Metro Toronna
Would insist, "I can cuss if I wanna.
    I don't use dirty words
    Like you c — — — s — — — — — — t — — — —
But some day I am f — — — — — — well gonna!"

K.M.

The geologists argue in chorus
That the dinosaurs lived long before us.
　　But when walking down Yonge
　　You can still fall among
Some inebriate Torontosoreass.

H.O.

A fat, willing girl of Toronto,
When asked, said, "Of course, if you want to,"
　　And quickly reclined
　　In a posture designed
To facilitate climbing up onto.

A.J.M. Smith

There was a young whore of East York
Who put herself quite out of work
    When, disgruntled with men,
    Crying, "Never again!"
She bunged herself up with a cork.

K.M.

A charming young maid from Don Mills
Used to walk about naked for thrills.
    Said the vicar, "I blush
    When I look at her brush
But will lift up mine eyes to the hills."

H.O.

An impotent man in Port Credit
Used shot in his pencil to lead it.
    He enjoyed a few fucks
    With some upended ducks
But drew blanks with the ladies, who fled it.

H.O.

An old lady, from near Mississauga,
Was in love with a seasonal logger.
    "Though he cannot be here
    For ten months of the year,
Still, I love him — the silly old bugger!"

K.M.

After climbing the Hamilton Mt.
This broad cools herself in the ft.
    With a high-pressure spout
    Which she works in and out
As she murmurs, ecstatic, "Who's ct.!"

K.M.

There was an old man of St. Catharines
Who would drive, although subject to fatharines,
    Which gave all the folks
    Palpitations and strokes
And, on frequent occasions, the shatharines.

K.M.

A lad from Niagara Falls
Had a pair of spectacular balls
    Which he kept in condition
    For non-stop emission —
Inspired, no doubt, by the Falls!

K.M.

A priest in Niagara Falls
Inadvertently swallowed his balls,
    Thus attracting to prayer
    All the birds of the air
In response to his falsetto calls.

H.O.

Comes a broad to this orgy in Brampton,
With a chastity underpiece clamped on;
    Then she raffles the key
    And displays, vulgarly,
Where the price of her virtue is stamped on.

K.M.

A psychology student of Galt
Used to line her vagina with salt.
    "It's much better in bed
    Than is pepper," she said,
"Which is apt to disturb the 'gestalt'."

K.M.

There was an old granny of Guelph
Who played with a jolly old elph,
    Which she coddled and kept
    Till he died. Then she wept
And thereafter just played with herselph.

K.M.

An aging old pansy from Guelph
Was finally laid on the shelph,
    Where he thought back in time
    To his lecherous prime
And nostalgically played with himthelph.

H.O.

A persuasive young fellow of Kitchener
Turned his charm on his lady, bewitchener;
    Though indifferent to much
    Of black magic, and such,
He was really intent on the nitchener.

K.M.

A virgin outside Waterloo
Was determined to stay that way too.
    She armoured her tail
    With a sixteen-inch nail
And sealed her vagina with glue.

H.O.

A bright little maid in St. Thomas
Discovered a suit of pyjhomas.
    Said the maiden, "Well, well!
    Whose they are I can't tell,
But I'm sure these pyjhomas St Mhomas."

ANON.

An expectant young maid of St. Thos.
Sued her lover for breach of his pros.
    "An example," she claimed,
    "And in principle, aimed
At protecting the rights of us mos."

K.M.

67

There was a professor of Chatham
Who had an affair with an atom.
 The result of coition
 Was nuclear fission. . . .
There was a professor of Chatham.

H.O.

Three bawdy young women of Chatham,
Whose motto was, "Up, girls, and at 'em!,"
 Could never recall,
 With their babies and all,
Just which of their guys had begat 'em.

K.M.

A mechanic from near Holland Landing
Felt the surge of his urge so demanding,
 He assembled the few
 Sexy girls that he knew
And he ravished the lot, notwithstanding!

K.M.

On the soft, sunny sands near Washago,
Whither artists both virile and gay go,
 One can see every day
 Such erotic display,
I suspect, come the summer, I may go.

K.M.

There was a young lady of Barrie
Whom everyone wanted to marry.
　　But Tom made her sick
　　And she didn't like Dick
And a very nith boy cornered Harry.

H.O.

An expensive young tart of Orillia
Has a hundred perversions to thrillia.
　　After only two weeks
　　Of her oral techniques,
"You'll be all over come, when I billia."

K.M.

Said a prostitute down from Orillia,
"If I had your address I could billia;
    Or cash I take too;
    Even Chargex will do;
But you'd better pay up or I'll killia."

H.O.

An impulsive young man from Muskoka
Sat down to a game of strip poka.
    His jacket and tie
    Fell to pairs — aces high,
And his trousers he lost to a joka.

H.O.

There was an old man of Port Sydney
With a most undependable kidney,
    Thus enhancing the chance
    He would pee in his pance —
So he should have worn diapers, didney!

K.M.

An airman in bleak Killaloe,
Threw each of his girls in a stoe
    When, in uniform decked
    And with member erect,
He'd come at them, from out of the bloe.

K.M.

A sensuous lass of North Bay,
Not afraid to be laid in the hay,
    Gave it all without shame,
    Till at last she became,
So to speak, in the family way.

K.M.

There was a young man of Eau Claire
Who had an affair with a bear,
    But the surly old brute
    With a snap of her snoot
Left him only one ball and some hair.

ANON.

Thought a tadpole of upper Temagami,
"I foresee even less than monogamy
    'Cause I hear that the male
    Must surrender his tail —
Which will *not* make a lusty good frogami."

K.M.

On Sunday the elders of Timmins
Are happy at church singing hym-ns;
    The rest of the week
    Their pleasure they seek
Relaxing with wine and with wimmins.

Anne E. Anderson, Victoria, B.C.

At Timmins, a miner, ill-fated,
Would avoid safety clothes, insulated,
    Which down in the pit
    Didn't matter a bit
Till he came out at night — copperplated!

Mrs. Don Gale, Leamington, Ont.

A compliant young maid from Timiskaming
Discovered much more than a kisscaming.
    So she forewarned the lout
    He would have to pull out
Just in order, she pleaded, to misskaming.

H.O.

A torrid old tart of Timiskaming
Was so skilful, no partner could miss coming,
    And Saturday nights
    Were suffused in delights
As her clients exploded in bliss coming.

K.M.

A pubescent young lady of Hearst
Had a passion for firm liverwurst,
    Which at least was as good
    As the laggards who would
Enter only as far as they durst.

K.M.

A notorious harlot of Hearst
In the foibles of men is well versed;
    Reads a sign at the head
    Of her well-rumpled bed:
"Here the customer always comes first!"

ANON.

A hag wanders 'round Kapuskasing,
Each man she encounters embracing.
    Although blatantly nude
    She is hard to elude,
Coz you can't tell which way she is facing.

H.O.

A virgin from 'round Copper Cliff
Was eternally wondering if —
    Till at last, losing strength,
    She submitted at length,
And complained that the price was too stiff.

H.O.

On the Island by name Manitoulin
A chief, just to stop any foolin',
    Padlocked each of his squaws
    Into chastity drawers,
So that now there's no touchin' — just droolin'.

H.O.

During wintertime up at the Sault
It is chilly — there's nothing to dault;
 So they cope with the freeze
 Like the birds and the bees
And the birthrate goes up quite a fault.

H.O.

'Twas a lusty young lad from the Sault,
Who would ask all the girls, "Do you scrault?"
 When he once, just for fun,
 Propositioned a nun,
He was stunned by her gentle, "I dault!"

K.M.

A student at Sault Ste. Marie
Said, "Spelling is all Greek to me,
 Till they learn to spell 'Soo'
 Without any 'u'
Or an 'a' or an 'l' or a 't'!"

ANON.

There's no colder spot than White River
In the season Québecois call hiver.
 As the weather gets horrider
 Some move off to Florida,
Some screw and some drink and some shi-shiver.

H.O.

In the winter, up near Moosonee,
This old guy once related to me,
    As per local advice
    He could squirt only ice
Any time he attempted to pee.

K.M.

A maid from the town Thunder Bay
Was a hell of a wonderful lay;
    She would practise coition
    In any position
And willingly do it all day.

H.O.

A virgin who lives in Kenora
Has every man kneeling befora;
    But anxious to please,
    They should rise from their knees
And down and debauch and deflora.

H.O.

'Twas a prissy young missy named Laura
Who was had by a lad from Kenora,
    But the fit was so tight
    That, though try as he might,
He just couldn't do anything fora.

K.M.

THE PRAIRIES

In that Province of God, Manitoba,
Dwelt a lady more senile than sober,
    And, often confused
    By the words that she used,
Called her poodle a pinschermandober.

H.O.

'Neath the kilts of the Winnipeg pipers
They wear, I suspect, furry diapers,
    Coz at twenty below
    They need something, you know,
To keep off the frost from old Priapus.

H.O.

There was once a young Winnipeg maid
Who, the very first time she was laid,
    Became frigid, I'm told,
    " 'Cause it's too bloody cold
At the corder of Portage add Baid!"

K.M.

An outdoorsman of St. Boniface
Was imbued with a love of "la chasse",
    And especially in spring,
    It would make his heart sing
Just to think of a good piece of venison, or
    pheasant (or duck, maybe . . .) *K.M.*

A wet-nurse of Portage la Prairie
Has a bosom both massive and hairy.
    Nonetheless, since eighteen
    She's provided a clean
And productive and portable dairy.

K.M.

There was a young bridegroom of Brandon
With a bride both reserved and demandin'.
    She succumbed in the end,
    With the help of a friend
In a wild, orgiastic abandon.

K.M.

A pretentious young fellow from Brandon
Thought ceremony nothing to stand on.
    But the girl he accosted
    Remarked, somewhat frosted,
"Take your hand off what you got your hand on."

H.O.

Une fille, très jolie, de Dauphin
N'utilise que Chablis dans le bain,
    And some vigorous boys,
    With whose help she enjoys
(A son gout éxotique) coq-au-vin.

K.M.

During winter, up north in The Pas,
An acquaintance once told me, in as,
    "They go naked," he said,
    "Up to ten in a bed!"
An example of life in the ras.

K.M.

I remember a lad from Saskatchewan
Who kept looking for places to pat you on;
    Down there and up here,
    And by proxy, the queer,
With a hand-shaped settee which he sat you on!

K.M.

Said a pander who lived in Saskatchewan,
"You haven't a hope if it's snatchewan,
    Coz the ladies 'round here
    Can run fleeter than deer;
But for twenty-five bucks I will catchewan."

H.O.

A bashful young girl from Fort San
May pretend that she can't but she can —
    In a bed, on the turf,
    Upside down, soixante-neuf,
With any available man.

H.O.

A lecher from old Saskatoon
Did all his best leching at noon,
    Till he made rather free
    With the Rose of Tralee
By the Light of the Silvery Moon.

K.M.

For its civil defence, Saskatoon
Raised a forty-man naval platoon.
    When they asked for a grant
    They were told "No, you can't,
Since your needs are, at best, picayune."

J.P. Slugworthy

A queer from around Saskatoon
Said, "I reckon I'm leaving here soon;
　　For all of the fairies
　　Out here on the prairies,
I might as well live on the moon."

H.O.

Prince Albert is surely God's Acre:
For here, hewn on stone from his Maker,
　　Was our great Bill of Rights
　　Carried down from the heights
By His prophet, John G. Diefenbaker.

F.P. Hughes, Hawkesbury, Ont.

A peevish young girl of Batoche
Tried to pee in her brother's galosh,
　　Pretty mad, 'cause "The swine
　　Did it straight into mine,
But with me it came out all awash!"

K.M.

A stripper who came from Regina
Would reject all attempts to refina,
　　Like the time in Glace Bay,
　　With a gutsy "Hey! Hey!"
She displayed, I'm afraid, her gluteus maximus.

K.M.

A queer long ago in Regina
Was booked for assaulting a mina;
 Though not, I should add,
 Some cute little lad,
But a pick-wielding fat fortynina.

H.O.

A frigid young flapper from Bender
Suspected that nothing could sender,
 Till one fall at a ball
 She went clean up the wall
When a hand from the band touched her gender.

H.O.

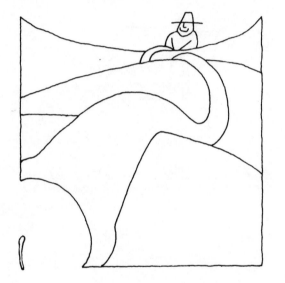

A fruiterer, out in Wascana,
Grew the world's most expansive banana.
    He could normally swell
    Way beyond Fort Qu'Appelle
And, when specially roused, to Montana!

K.M.

A puzzled old judge in Swift Current
Couldn't figure a proper deterrent;
    For the culprits he saw
    Who were breaking the law
Looked the same as the people who weren't!

Charles Moreau, Kingston, Ont.

In the woodlands around Maple Creek
A troop of boy scouts took a leak,
    Which intrusion of waste
    Almost ruined the taste
Of the sugaring-off for a week.

H.O.

There was a young man of Moose Jaw
Who wanted to meet Bernard Shaw;
    When they questioned him, "Why?"
    He made no reply
But sharpened an axe and a saw.

ANON.

A medicine man from the Sioux
Used to colour his features bright blioux.
   When asked why he dyed,
   "My squaw," he replied,
"Likes to look at the sky when we scrioux."

H.O.

Now what in the world shall we dioux
With the bloody and murderous Sioux,
   Who some time ago
   Took an arrow and bow
And raised such a hellabelioux?

Eugene Field

The "bloody and murderous Sioux"
As a stereotype is untrioux;
   Though they did take a stand
   In defence of their land,
Making quite a to-dioux — wouldn't yioux?

K.M.

An experienced girl of Alberta
Was convinced that no pecka could hurta,
   Though she felt some unease
   When invited to squeeze
On the province's champion squirta.

K.M.

An eccentric old maid from Alböethe
Developed a passion for Gerther,
    Ploughing all the way through
    Faust parts one and tough
And sorrowing now with young Werta.

H.O.

A spinster from Medicine Hat
On guard just "for thee" duly sat;
    And the Yanks were afraid
    To encroach or invade —
She was 54° 40′ and fat.

J.P. Slugworthy

Big Robert from Medicine Hat
Thought he had the procedure down pat;
    But pinned to the wall
    He mistimed his withdrawal —
Thus it was Little Bob was begat.

H.O.

There's a damsel in Medicine Hat
Who will warn all her gentlemen that
    "When I'm toute exposée
    At the height of the play,
I am never quite sure where I'm at!"

K.M.

An ecdysiast in Fort Macleod,
Who was really superbly endowed,
    Would enticingly bare
    A most ravishing pair,
To the frenzied applause of the crowd.

K.M.

At a gathering near Fort Macleod,
This whisper, close by in the crowd:
    "I do not object,
    Now you're fully erect,
But kindly don't do it so loud."

H.O.

A bronc at the Calgary Stampede
From perversity rather than need
    Disdained to attack
    The young man on its back —
Merely stood in the middle and peed.

H.O.

A Calgary cowboy named Pete
Was put down by them western elite —
    So he moved to Quebec —
    Said "Mais oui, what the heck,
Now I'm rodeo champ of St. Tite!"

Joyce Hibbert, Drummondville, Que.

Said an amorous husband of Red Deer,
Breathing low to his wife, "Come to bed, dear."
   Muttered she, "What the hell,
   Yes, I may just as well
'Cause I'm thirty days over my sched, dear."

K.M.

In her garden an Edmonton maid
Hollered out that she needed a spade,
   But was quite thunder-struck
   When she called for a fork —
And was promptly and lustily laid!

H.O.

One Edmonton man that I knew
Was a pet, but he hadn't a clue!
   Apprehensive in bed,
   He was frequently said
To persuade the young maid to *un*screw.

K.M.

At a masquerade near Athabaska
I hadn't the nerve to unmaska.
   But now, I suppose,
   I've removed all her clothes —
Now it might be all right, so alaska.

H.O.

An Eskimo in Athabaska
Let his igloo to friends from Alaska.
When they said, "Does your spouse
Go along with the house?"
He replied, "I don't know, but I'll aska."

Mavor Moore, Toronto, Ont.

In the seventeen hundreds in Banff
You wrote s with an f; fo the manfe
Waf a houfe, where to piff
Waf regarded amiff,
But leff fo than wetting your pantf.

John Reeves, Toronto, Ont.

An impatient young fellow of Banff
Would appear to have anff in hif panff—
    But 'twaf really a purge
    Of a fexual urge
Through a kind of Ft. Vituf'f Danff.

K.M.

Overheard down beside Lake Louise
Came her voice, wafting by on the breeze,
    "TAKE YOUR FINGER FROM THAT! . . .
    But I'll trade tit for tat
With the warmth of your hands upon these."

K.M.

At a golf course beside Lake Louise,
A lady too anxious to please
    Curled up in a ball
    And while offering all,
Was lambasted from one of the tees.

H.O.

A trapper of cold Fort McMurray
Must always make love in a hurry;
    "Well, I has to," he said,
    "They near shoots through the bed,
'Cause the end of me dingle is furry."

K.M.

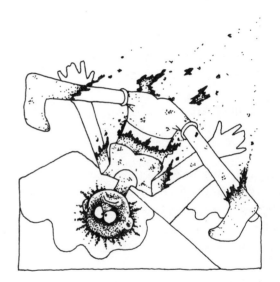

BRITISH COLUMBIA

In the Rockies a sturdy young guide
Used to take all the girls in his stride
    At the top of the pass,
    For he wanted his ass
With a true Continental Divide.

K.M.

An incestuous lady I knew
Climbed the Rockies to witness the view.
    They reminded her rather,
    She said, of her father,
Her brothers and great-uncle too.

H.O.

A ruthless young man from B.C.
Would only perform for a fee.
    "See it this way," he said,
    "They just lie on the bed;
But think what it takes out of me."

H.O.

A tourist with prizes from Bisley
Was sure he could handle things isley.
    With his gun he set forth
    To discomfit the north —
He was eaten for lunch by a grisley.

H.O.

Said a beauty from British Columbia
To her boyfriend, "How stupidly dumbia;
    I'm sure that my chest
    Is the best in the west
And so why are you sucking the thumbia?"

H.O.

She kept her libido concealed,
This passionate lady of Field,
    As an idealist
    With a will to resist,
And another to gracefully yield.

K.M.

There are few who would screw or dispute any
Of the claims of some dames from the Kootenay
    As to moistness and size —
    Although doubts could arise
Were they open to critical scrutiny.

K.M.

The ghost that inhabits Fort Steele
Is really alarmingly real,
    Chasing ladies for sport
    Round the walls of the fort
With a cock like a large conger eel.

H.O.

A voyeur from Cranbrook, B.C.,
Had the strangest perversion, oui, oui;
    He got all his kicks
    Out of pendulous pricks
While watching the RCM pee.

H.O.

A bisexual person of Trail
Would prefer to be robustly male,
    And enjoy the sensation
    The right operation
Could probably fully en-tail.

K.M.

At Radium Springs on vacation
A tourist absorbed radiation.
    Which led in due course
    To a potent new force —
He could couple without penetration!

H.O.

A fellow from Radium Springs
Built a pair of magnificent wings;
    But he didn't have oughta
    Flown low over wata —
A duck hunter shot off his things.

H.O.

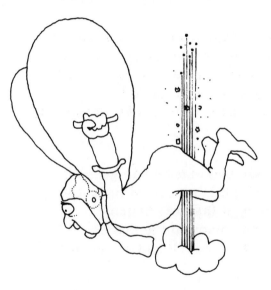

A brave from around Craigellachie
Succeeded a white squaw to catchie.
    Her scalp he disdained
    Because he explained
That he lusted far more for her snatchie.

H.O.

This bordello outside Craigellachie
Faltered not in pursuit of the buckie.
    Since it first was begun
    It has followed the one
Simple dictum, "No payee, no fachie."

K.M.

Hip, hooray, for the ladies of Sicamous,
Be they russet, brunette or auricomous,
    And whose ripe womanhood
    With its attributes, would
Be enough to make Calvin polygamous!

K.M.

A commodious maid from McBride
Had a cleft over half a foot wide.
    If you fancied, 'tis said,
    You could shove in your head
And utter foul sayings inside.

H.O.

A girl wanders over Moose Heights
Wearing only a pair of silk tights.
   Though no bloody use
   At exciting the moose,
All the farmers for miles she delights.

H.O.

An exceptional lad of Quesnel,
My old granny would frequently tell,
   So perfected the swing
   Of his pendulous thing,
He could ding with his dong, like a bell.

K.M.

When you walk around Kamloops, you pant,
For everything there's on a slant;
    Not a crook in the town,
    But with hills up and down
People try to go straight, but they can't.

Donald Bishop, Barrie, Ont.

A middleaged man of Kamloops
Used to ravish his women in groups,
    Long ago. But today,
    To his utmost dismay,
After two at the most, he just droops.

K.M.

A farmer from Lake Okanagan
Had to carry his cock in a wagon,
    Coz the fruits of his trade
    Weren't the sort to be laid,
Yet they left a perpetual jagon.

H.O.

I know a young fellow of Vernon
Who is seeking the ultimate turn-on;
    He has not found it yet,
    But I'm willing to bet
That he's having a ball while he's learnin'.

K.M.

A virgin of Vernon, B.C.
Was resolved to be raped by a tree!
    She was dropped from a plane
    Over forest terrain
And on landing was heard to say, "whee-E-E-E!"

K.M.

A gaudy young girl of Kelowna
Does her act in a sexy kimono;
    She tastefully ripples
    Her tumescent nipples —
With lipstick all 'round her corona.

K.M.

Some intriguing sex modes of Penticton,
Although seldom the kind to convict on,
> Do include one or two
> Of the sort that a few
Of the townsfolk are overly strict on.

K.M.

There was a young tart from the Fraser
So cool that no fella could phase 'er,
> Till that logger she met —
> After that I forget
If he flays, sways, dismays or just lays 'er.

K.M.

There was a young lady of Spuzzum,
Who harboured *two* snakes in her buzzum.
> She explained, "It's my fate
> That I overlactate —
So I just drops 'em in, and they duzzum!"

K.M.

The breasts of two broads of Coquitlam
Were so stunning one couldn't belittlam.
> Their perfection and size
> Made a lot of the guys
Uncontrollably drool, and bespittlam.

K.M.

A flat-chested tart from Vancouver
Took silicon shots to improve her.
    But alas the effex
    Were concave, not convex,
Which utterly spoilt her whore d'oeuver.

H.O.

There was an old prude of Vancouver,
So frigid that no one could mouver,
    Till one lad did the trick
    With a dip of the wick
In a special Vancouver manoeuvre.

K.M.

A pastrycook down on his luck
Became a Vancouver Canuck.
　　Though he wasn't so hot
　　When he slapped in a shot,
He was dandy at icing the puck.

H.O.

A stereo jock in Vancouver
Had a two-channel, fifteen-inch woofer,
　　Overloading his wife,
　　In their sexual life,
With an output sufficient for two of 'er.

K.M.

An illiterate lass from Vancouver,
When informed it was not "horses doover",
 Could not muster her nerve
 To request the hors d'oeuvre,
So had soup as a saving manoeuvre.

Mrs. V. Sinclair-Smith, Kootenay Bay, B.C.

Vancouver is growing, they say,
So fast that there'll soon come a day
 It'll annex Toronto,
 Then, turning 'round pronto,
Obligingly take in L.A.

Joyce Hibbert, Drummondville, Quebec.

A masochist at Simon Fraser
Castrated himself with a razor;
  But managed despite
  To rekindle his light
By the use of two eggs and a laser.

H.O.

An apartment outside New Westminster
Housed an aging and desperate spinster
  Who was longing to fool
  With the caretaker's tool —
But he never would hold it aginster.

K.M.

There was a young girl of Victoria
Who was whooped by an Indian warria,
    Much later at leisure
    Recalling with pleasure
That state of pacific euphoria.

K.M.

Victoria winters, they say,
Are as balmy as England in May.
    But occasional fogs
    Are so dense that the dogs
Ask the bloodhounds to show them the way.

Arthur MacFarlane, Moncton, N.B.

One Sunday, a harlot named Gloria
Established a beat in Victoria.
    Next day in her whoredom
    She died out of boredom;
Hence on Mundi 'twas sic transit gloria.

H.O.

If you're out in the straits they call Georgia,
And a mermaid starts swimming towargia,
    Insist that you think
    She's a sweet salmon-pink,
And explain, "I just cannot afforgia."

H.O.

In the Klondike a story is told
Of the mountains encrusted with gold;
    But of all them thar hills,
    It was big Diamond Lil's
That the miners most liked to behold.

H.O.

Said the fair-haired Rebecca of Klondike,
"Of you I'm exceedingly fond, Ike.
    To prove I adore you
    I'll dye, darling, for you
And be a brunette, not a blonde, Ike."

ANON.

A curmudgeonous miner from Dawson
Was forever blasphemin' and cawson
   A lecherous bitch
   With a hand with an itch
For the private preserves of his pawson.

H.O.

A bestial lady of Whitehorse
Spent a lifetime in search of the right horse;
   "When I want to," she said,
   "Take a stallion to bed,
On the whole, I'd prefer a quite light horse."

K.M.

In Whitehorse the story is told
Of a prude running nude through the cold,
   Saying life in the Yukon
   Was something to pukon
And wishing to be a gatefold.

H.O.

An Eskimo up in Inuvik
Was richly endowed and to pruvik
   He harpooned a seal
   Which so loved the feel
That nothing on earth will remuvik.

H.O.

Though they say Baffin Land is quite pretty
Its location's a bit of a pity.
   'Twould be nice to up anchor
    And tow it by tanker
And moor it outside Quebec city.
H.O.

A hotblooded young esquimau
Tried to screw his beloved in the snau.
   But on finding it froze
    He abruptly aroze
Saying "Since I can't come, I must gau."
H.O.

To an Eskimo living up north
Declared the Almighty, "Come forth!"
    But according to myth
    The poor fellow came fyfth
And occasioned the Almighty's wrath.

H.O.

An Eskimo got quite a shock
When a seal that he carved out of rock
    Grew bored of just basking
    And, not even asking,
Maliciously bit off his cock.

H.O.

It is peaceful up north — that is true,
But the folk have their privations too,
    Coz at sixty below
    The bananas don't grow
And even the movies are blue.

H.O.

In the lands of the icy north west
Lived a maid with a dolorous breast;
    She had one nipple lost —
    Bitten off by the frost . . .
Or so she preferred to protest.

H.O.

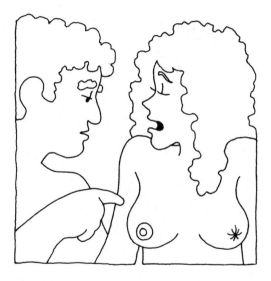

A sensitive youth from Pine Point
Had his nose rather put out of joint
    When its curious tip
    Was held fast in the grip
Of the thing that he hoped to anoint.

H.O.

A Yellowknife miner named Dan
Baked all of his bread in a pan.
    It was always like lead,
    So he carved it instead;
Now it's Eskimo art in Japan.

Catherine Stephenson, Brantford, Ont.

CANADIAN THEMES AND PERSONALITIES

Most Canadians happen to dwell
Near the forty-ninth north parallel,
    And observing the States,
    Offer thanks to the fates
That old Brock and his boys fought so well.

H.O.

On the ice with the U.S.S.R.
Team Canada's better by far,
    Because views au contraire
    Are too heavy to bear —
They must be, and therefore they are.

H.O.

The hockey star melted in tears
When the ref gave him twenty-five years,
    For boarding and necking,
    Rough play and cross-checking
And hooking spectators' brassieres.

H.O.

To our past hockey greats, drink a toast,
For their names are forgotten — almost;
    Save their glories of old
    Which in stories are told
Every Saturday night, ghost to ghost.

H.O.

The female Canadian beaver
Displays an unlikely spring fever
    When she cuts down a spruce
    And converts it to use
As a sort of vibrator-cum-lever.

H.O.

The Canadian beaver female
Is a prospect before which I pale;
    But her mate I suppose
    Through his spectacles rose
Sees simply a cute piece of tail.

H.O.

An Indian squaw on the loose
Was ravished one day by a moose.
    But what is much worse,
    She now has to nurse
A four-footed horny papoose.

H.O.

A trout breaks the surface for flies
Or deep on the lake bottom lies.
    But Canadian fish
    Have no choice what they wish —
When their mercury rises they rise.

H.O.

A miner out looking for rocks
Came down with a dose of the pox,
    Which he argues was due
    To a loose caribou
When in fact 'twas a cute silver fox.

H.O.

The Great Lakes are the world's largest source
Of "fresh" water — assuming of course
    That fresh you define
    As a sea of urine
All awash with green algae — or wource.

H.O.

We started with colonization
Proceeding to Confederation.
    We've fought a few wars
    And now take a pause
For nation identification.

F.P. Hughes, Hawkesbury, Ont.

The passing of Bill 22
Has split our two cultures, it's true.
    So now when we meet
    In silence complete
We just eat and we drink and we screw.

H.O.

If some are perpetually high,
It's Canadian whiskey — that's why.
    Though in terms of performance
    It expedites dormance —
It's harder to come through the rye.

H.O.

As he strolled on the water, our mod
Prime Minister mumbled, "How odd!
    My two sons were born
    On Christmas day morn,
Which makes me one better than God."

H.O.

A glutton who went out to dine
Drank a quart of Canadian wine.
    He was later found pissed
      On the critical list,
But the doctors predict he'll do fine.

H.O.

Of greatness this world has its store —
Leonardo and Shakespeare and Shaw,
    Voltaire, Joan of Arc,
      Mendeleev and Bach,
Bobby Hull, Esposito and Orr.

H.O.

Old Dief's oratorical pride
Flows on like a torrent's high tide —
　　A great river bed
　　One foot deep at the head,
At the mouth almost half a mile wide.

H.O.

Mr. Stanfield's conservative stance
Comes across unappealing perchance;
　　But lose, draw or win,
　　He sticks close to the skin
And many have Stan's on their pance.

H.O.

Although he will do you no harm
The spectre of General Montcalm
　　On long summer nights
　　Wanders Abraham's Heights
Bidding someone to sound the alarm.

H.O.

Macdonald won great reputation
Giving birth to our glorious nation;
　　But there's rumours that say
　　In his cups Sir John A.
Fathered much more than Confederation.

H.O.

"**O** Canada" let us all sing
Till the birds in the forest take wing.
   I know that the words
   Were meant for the birds,
But it's better than "God save the King".

H.O.

Hugh Oliver, born in Epsom, England, came to Canada in 1966. He is editor, author (of chemistry books and of General Publishing's *The Art of Aluminum Foil*), record lyric writer (the Beatles did backing music for one) and sculptor.

$\mathbf{K}$eith MacMillan, born in Toronto into a family that knew $\frac{6}{8}$ from $\frac{2}{4}$, wrote, directed and acted in musical comedies at University of Toronto before embarking on careers as CBC radio music producer, pioneer of Canadian LP recording, and promoter of Canadian music —and other Canadiana.

Roy Condy was born in Dagenham, England, and came to Canada as a child. He went to the Ecole des Beaux Arts in Montreal. After doing time as a go-fer in an advertising art studio, he worked in the audiovisual dept. of Sir George Williams University and as supervisor of the art dept. in a publishing house. Now he freelances.